D0857943

Driftwood

Stories Picked Up Along the Shore

Driftwood

Stories Picked Up Along the Shore

Paintings and Companion Stories by Howard Sivertson

Lake Superior Port Cities Inc.
Duluth, Minnesota
2008

©2008 by Howard Sivertson

All rights reserved. No part of this publication may be reproduced or transmitted in any
form or by any means, electronic or mechanical, including photocopying, recording or any
information storage and retrieval system, without permission in writing from the publisher.

First edition published May 2008 by

LAKE SUPERIOR PORT CITIES INC.
P.O. Box 16417
Duluth, Minnesota 55816-0417
USA
1-888-BIG LAKE (888-244-5253) • www.lakesuperior.com
Publishers of *Lake Superior Magazine* and *Lake Superior Travel Guide*

5 4 3 2 1

Library of Congress Cataloging-In-Publication Data

Sivertson, Howard, 1930-
    Driftwood : stories picked up along the shore :
paintings and companion stories / by Howard Sivertson.
        p. cm.
    Includes bibliographical references.
    ISBN 978-0-942235-91-3
    1. Superior, Lake, Region – History – Anecdotes. 2. Superior, Lake, Region –
History – Pictorial works. I. Title.
F552 .S56 2008
977.4'9 – dc22   2008007960

Printed in Canada

    Editors: Paul L. Hayden, Konnie LeMay
    Printer: Friesens Book Division, Winnipeg, Manitoba

This book is dedicated to Elaine

977.49
Siv

Blue Alpine $94.95

GERMANTOWN COMMUNITY LIBRARY
WITHDRAWN
GERMANTOWN, WI 53022

Nipigon

Ontario

Rossport

Port
Coldwell

Ontario

Kam River

Port Arthur

Thunder
Bay

Fort William

Pie Island

Pic River

Boundary Waters

Pigeon River

McKellar
Point

Spar Island

Lake
Superior

Isle Royale

Grand Portage

Susie
Islands

Michipicoten River

Minnesota

Hovland

Grand Marais

Lutsen

Michipicoten Island

Gargantua Harbour

Tofte

Eagle River

Copper Harbor

Agawa River

Beaver Bay

Montreal River

Two Harbors

Hancock

Houghton

Duluth

Bayfield

Ontonagon

Whitefish Point

Washburn

La Pointe

L'Anse

Superior

Brule
River

Chequamegon
Bay

Pointe Aux Pins

Ashland

Marquette

Sault Ste. Marie

Wisconsin

Munising

Michigan

Table of Contents

Acknowledgements

Arrowhead Library System
Dr. Timothy Cochrane – Superintendent
   Grand Portage National Monument
Carol Desain
Cook County Historical Society
Tom Gale
Grand Portage National Monument
Paul and Cindy Hayden and the staff at
   Lake Superior Port Cities Inc.
Thom Holden
Isle Royale National Park Service

C. Patrick Labadie
Lake County Historical Society
Donn Larson
David Lightwood
James R. Marshall
Old Fort William Librarians
Rolf O. Peterson
St. Louis County Historical Society
Thunder Bay Historical Museum
Brian Tofte

Introduction

Lake Superior was discovered by explorer/adventurers looking for a shorter trade route to the Far East from Europe. Columbus stumbled onto North America in several attempts to find the Far East by going west, the opposite direction from normal trade routes, back when the world was considered to be flat.

John Cabot and son, Sebastian, followed close in his wake exploring every nook and cranny of Labrador, Nova Scotia and Greenland, looking for the passage to Asia. About 100 years later, Henry Hudson thought that he had found the route to riches when he sailed into Hudson's Bay and paid for his mistake with his life.

About the same time in 1608, Samuel de Champlain with his protégé, Ètienne Brûlé, arrived in the St. Lawrence River Valley, previously discovered by Jacques Cartier in 1534. Champlain sent the young Brûlé to live with the Huron Indians to explore the country west of the St. Lawrence and to learn the language and customs of the people.

In 1613, Brûlé's Indian friends showed him Lake Superior, the first white man to gaze over that giant body of water. Fresh water. Not salty at all. Brûlé was the first white man to venture with his Huron companions in bark canoes along the north shore to the western end. They were looking for a route to salt water and the Pacific Ocean.

Of course, he didn't find his objective, but in the process opened the Great Lakes area to a fur trade that lasted for more than 250 years. Exploration and mining for copper, silver, gold and iron ore began about 1730. Lake Superior had become the objective and not just the way to somewhere else. Men settled the shores to work the mines, harvest the fish and lumber and to build the cities.

Their mostly undocumented adventures leave much to our imaginations. Occasionally we can find bits and pieces of their colorful lives, and by putting the pieces together we get an idea of just what their days were like.

Some left evidence of their exploits in diaries, journals and business records from which historians interpreted this area's history.

Some left evidence for archaeologists and beachcombers to find. Arrowheads and pottery shards from early Indian cultures; clay pipes, beads and implements from the fur trade days; broken planks, ribs and sail cloth from early wooden ships; boom logs, chains and pulpwood sticks from logging days; net corks, floats and buoys from the commercial fishing era – all can be found amongst the driftwood, half buried in sand or peeking out from under wild beach roses and peas at the berm line of Lake Superior's ubiquitous beaches.

But all the records, diaries and artifacts left behind account for only a very small part of our history. The rest is left to our imaginations and educated guesses. For instance: In searching through early records of the fur trade business, scholarly historians found barely enough information to compile a few paragraphs about fur trader Louis Denis de La Ronde and the first decked-over schooner built on Lake Superior. "The earliest known decked vessel to sail the Great Lake (Superior) was *La Rondes*, built about 1735 at Pointe Aux Pins. It was twenty five tons burden and carried at least two sails." *Grace Lee Nute – Lake Superior.*

A brief description of its mission in the copper mining venture followed, but not much else to satisfy my curiosity. What did it look like? What were her day-to-day experiences searching for and mining copper on one of the world's most dangerous lakes? Was it also used in the fur trade with the Indians? What finally happened to it?

One day in 2004, while beachcombing Grace Harbor on Isle Royale, I spotted a chunk of wood, large enough to sit on and have lunch, sticking out of the sand near the crest of the beach. I had time to look more closely at it while eating a sandwich and noticed paint chips embedded in the weathered grain of the wood. After moving sand and gravel away from it with a piece of driftwood, I exposed about 50 feet of a huge wooden ship's keel. Was it part of the *Cumberland, George M. Cox, Isle Royale, Dagmar* or another sunken or missing ship long before my time? What were her stories? The weather changed and the wind shifted, exposing my boat to the growing seas. I covered up the keel with sand and gravel and left the beach to hide the prize until I returned another day.

As archaeologists can reconstruct an ancient culture by studying its artifacts, historians can reconstruct events by studying bits and pieces of information found in archives or among the driftwood along Lake Superior's shores.

Some of the stories in this book are events from my personal experience that I felt important and interesting enough to preserve for future generations. Many of the stories are from historical events before my time and are the result of combing the archives for little known facts about major events, then applying the power of deduction and imagination to document how it may have looked.

I hope this book will be like a piece of driftwood you find along the shore and will arouse your curiosity to search for more of the colorful history of Lake Superior country.

– Howard Sivertson
Grand Marais, Minnesota
April 2008

Driftwood

In days of yore, driftwood covered Lake Superior's countless beaches. Dead trees floated down rivers to the open lake where they drifted with the wind until they were finally pushed ashore during a storm. They provided a handy source of firewood for lake dwellers throughout history.

Shipwrecks contributed their ribs, planks and contents to the driftwood piles in the 19th century when wooden sailing ships crashed into each other and the many rocks and reefs of the uncharted lake. Some of their tarred pieces can still be found buried in sand under beach peas and roses at the berm.

Until recently, Lake Superior was used as a dumping ground for settlers living around the lake and for ships at sea. Anything not wanted was thrown into the endless, bottomless lake. Some of those articles have become valuable artifacts in the eyes of the beachcomber.

From the early 1900s until recent times, a relatively new source of driftwood joined the others. Saw logs and pulpwood sticks that escaped from giant rafts, being towed by tugs from the United States and Canadian river mouths, broke free in lake storms to roam the lake until they got waterlogged and sank or got washed up on beaches. The white pine saw logs were on their way to Ashland and Duluth via rafting tugs to be made into lumber. Poplar, balsam and spruce rafts were towed to paper mills in Ashland.

Beachcombers of all sorts salvaged the white pine logs and pulpwood sticks for construction projects and firewood. Some made up their own rafts or loaded their boats with wood that they'd sell back to the logging companies or the mills.

The piles of driftwood are almost gone from the lake's beaches today. Some random logs, 50 to 90 years old, can still be found in useable condition. New environmental laws limit the amount of precious junk available to beachcombers, but the hunt for artifacts, driftwood and stuff is still a fascinating activity. As is the search for these stories.

Lake Superior's First Decked-Over Vessel

Before Louis Denis, sieur de la Ronde, had his schooner built at Pointe Aux Pins near Sault Ste. Marie, Ontario, in 1735, only bark canoes navigated Lake Superior, carrying furs and trade goods along her shores.

The first French fur traders arrived by bark canoes at Chequamegon Bay about 1650 to trade with the Indians who had settled there in about 1500. Governor Vaudrevil of New France had a permanent trading post built there in 1718. In 1727, he appointed la Ronde as manager of the post and all Lake Superior trade. He also gave instructions to keep an eye out for signs of copper and other precious metals rumored to be lying about on the beaches.

La Ronde got along well with the Indians who confided in him the location of an island covered in copper and another island with golden beaches. La Ronde was also given permission to inspect the huge sacred copper boulder in the Ontonagon River. He decided to add mineral exploration and mining to his fur trading responsibilities and became the first white man to attempt mining on Lake Superior.

The 25-ton, two-masted schooner he had built at Point Aux Pins near Sault Ste. Marie was to help him explore for potential mining locations and haul copper and gold to the Sault and supplies to the mines.

I assume that la Ronde would immediately have checked out the obvious sources of his mining fever, the legendary floating copper island (Isle Royale) and the golden beaches of Caribou Island. It's also a fair assumption that he used his stout ship to haul furs eastward and trade goods westward from the Sault to his trading post at La Pointe on Chequamegon Bay.

Records show that he did mine copper at three locations on the south shore, but the lack of better mining technology and a supporting agricultural community made mining too risky and expensive. A war between the Sioux and Chippewa, followed by the French and Indian War, ended mining operations temporarily and the French regime, in North America, permanently.

In trying to imagine the subject for my painting of la Ronde's schooner, I considered her adventurous life on dangerous Lake Superior, caught in storms, stranding on reefs, lost in fog, loading and unloading at a mine location or at her wharf at La Pointe. I settled on what she would look like, becalmed at anchor in the harbor at Grand Marais, Michigan. His Indian friends, camped on the point, would surely have come to visit, to trade or just to chat about floating copper islands, golden beaches and the price of beaver at Michilimackinac.

Alexander Henry – From Fur Trading to Mining and Back

The fur trade in southern Canada lay dormant from 1756 to 1763 during the Seven Years War between France and England for possession of Canada. For several years after the English had won, the war, most Indian tribes along the traditional trade routes remained loyal to their allies, the French, and hostile to their enemies, the English. They threatened to kill any English traders caught in their territory.

Alexander Henry was the first Englishman to take the risk. With four canoes and 12 voyageurs he headed for Lake Superior, stopping for provisions at Fort Michilimackinac on the south shore of the Straits of Mackinac. While at the fort, he was caught up in a massacre intended to kill all Englishmen at the fort. Henry was the only Englishman to escape, thanks to a friendly Chippewa family who later adopted him. Disguised as an Indian man, he spent the next two years trapping in the Sault Ste. Marie upper Lake Michigan area with his adopted family.

In 1765, Henry was granted exclusive trading rights to Lake Superior by the new commandant of Fort Michilimackinac. He proceeded to Chequamegon Bay, on the big lake's south shore, where he built a trading post on La Pointe Island … probably the same site used by Louis Denis de la Ronde a few years earlier. After a successful season, he moved his operation to the mouth of the Michipicoten River on Lake Superior's east shore.

Alexander Henry became distracted from the fur business by raw copper lying about on the beaches. When the opportunity came to join in partnership with two other Englishmen with mining experience, he couldn't resist. Like la Ronde, they built a decked-over ship at Pointe Aux Pins along with a barge to be used in exploring and mining copper.

After their first attempt at mining on the Ontonagon River where copper was plentiful but too expensive to mine, Henry turned his ship to the east and north shores of the lake in hopes of finding a lode more easily accessible.

One of the rivers he explored was probably the Montreal River, illustrated in the painting, but to no avail. And so, the sloop was sold, the company disbanded and Alexander Henry entered the fur trade once more, earning fame and fortune in the territory as a partner in the North West Company.

Perilous Landing

Nowadays it would be dumber than foolhardy to paddle a 36-foot canoe, made of birch bark, loaded to the gunwales with 5,000 pounds of cargo, plus a crew of eight men, along the rugged north shore of Lake Superior from Sault Ste. Marie to Grand Portage. But the French Canadian voyageurs accomplished that remarkable feat for more than 200 years.

It took voyageur brigades about six days to make the trip, hauling out the canoes and camping ashore each night. Sand or gravel beaches, protected from heavy weather, were preferred campsites, safe enough to land, unload and haul out the fragile canoes.

Such beaches are common on the east shore from Sault Ste. Marie as far as Michipicoten River. But north and west of there the shoreline consists of rocks and precipitous cliffs interspersed with precious few beaches to accommodate canoe unloading. Voyageurs had their favorite beaches and usually tried to reach them by nightfall. Sometimes they had to paddle in heavy weather to get there, only to find landing and unloading precarious in the heavy surf. Canoes were paddled close to shore, and men jumped into waist-deep water to hold the canoe in position while others unloaded the cargo on shore. Then four men lifted the canoe from the water and carried it ashore. Tipped on its side it became their shelter for the night.

Sometimes canoes, cargoes and men were lost. The voyageurs felt that in the eyes of the tightfisted business partners, the most precious of the three were the canoes and cargo.

Sailing Home Through the Susie Islands

It wasn't mosquitoes, sore backs and hernias that attracted the young men from Montreal to become voyageurs. It wasn't the seemingly endless paddling and carrying tons of furs and trade goods across stormy lakes and hot bug-infested portages that lured them. Wine, women and song were the sirens of the farm boys from the St. Lawrence Valley, for the first time away from home and far from priests.

They left Montreal in May and after six weeks and 1,200 miles of grueling labor, paddling and carrying their tons of cargo for about 18 hours a day, they arrived at Grand Portage, tired but eager for the festivities that were to be their reward. But before they could join the fun, it would be another week of lugging 90-pound packs of hernia-inducing trade goods for nine miles uphill to Fort Charlotte on the Pigeon River, then lugging 90-pound packs of furs back down the Great Carrying Place to the stockade on the bay.

For the next week or two they partied, full out, with all the energy they could muster. During the day, the pork eaters from Montreal competed in all sorts of contests and games with the voyageurs of the northwest. In the evening, wine, women and song consumed what energy they had left.

Too soon, the fun and games were all over and it was time to load their canoes with two tons of furs and start the long, tiresome voyage back to Montreal and home. Six long weeks of paddling were ahead.

Lucky were the canoes that picked up a steady breeze from the southwest as they rounded Pointe Aux Chapeaux at the entrance to Grand Portage Bay. With a southwest wind directly astern, they could raise the blanket or canvas sail and coast along the shore until the breeze failed or changed direction. It was a good time to sit back and relax, light their pipes and reminisce about recent experiences at the Rendezvous. It's quite possible that a fair amount of teasing was directed toward the young novices who experienced the joys and pleasures of their first Rendezvous. But when they reached Montreal, I'm sure the rule "what happens at Rendezvous, stays at Rendezvous" prevailed.

Perseverance Rounding Pie Island – 1805

When a handful of Canadian fur traders decided to stop competing with each other and formed the North West Company in 1783, they decided to build a trading post at Grand Portage on the north shore of Lake Superior. Grand Portage was the midpoint between the southern shipping port of Montreal and the distant trading posts in northwest Canada.

Thirty-six-foot bark canoes were traditionally used to haul freight to and from Grand Portage and Sault Ste. Marie. They were fast and efficient in carrying the 90-pound packs of furs and trade goods and the small kegs of high wine, but were too small and fragile to carry heavier, awkward items like huge barrels of flour, bales of wire, cast iron cook stoves and farm animals and equipment.

The North West Company built the schooner *Athabaska,* then the *Otter,* to carry heavy goods between Grand Portage and the Sault. Their competitor, the XY Company, had the *Perseverance* built at Pointe Aux Pins just north of the Sault in 1801. The North West Company inherited the 80-ton sloop when it merged with the XY Company in 1804.

That same year, the North West Company moved its trading post from Grand Portage to Fort William at the mouth of the Kaministiquia River across the new border into Canada.

The *Perseverance* carried the bulk freight on Lake Superior until the War of 1812 when Captain Robert McCargoe of the North West Company burned her to keep her out of the hands of the Americans. I like to think it's possible that parts of her tarred and charred hull may still be hiding amongst the driftwood on the beach.

The painting shows her rounding Pie Island heading for Fort William on the Kaministiquia River in about 1805.

Hudson's Bay Company Outpost

In 1821, the North West Fur Company merged with the Hudson's Bay Company, drastically changing the fur trade routes in Canada. HBC shipped most of its freight, after the merger, on its traditional route across Canada to Hudson Bay. The Montreal-to-Fort William route was abandoned, except for a few express canoes that carried company partners and other dignitaries to Fort William and Fort Garry (Winnipeg). No longer the hub of the fur trade in North America, Fort William turned to commercial fishing to help support itself in its declining years.

HBC's Michipicoten River Post became the new link in the Lake Superior area fur trade because of its handy access to Moose Factory on James Bay in Hudson Bay, via the Michipicoten and Missanabie rivers. Indian trappers along the eastern shore carried their furs each spring to the Michipicoten, Pic or Sault Ste. Marie posts.

By the mid 1800s, HBC had established several outposts at traditional Indian encampments along the shore to better facilitate the trade, relieving Ojibway trappers of the long haul to distant posts. An outpost at Agawa River was established about 1823 that stayed in service until 1894. A clerk stayed on site to manage the post, sometimes all year, wintering over on what subsistence he could provide from his garden, fishing or hunting.

There is evidence that various tribal cultures used the campsites at the Pic, MacGregor Cove, Gargantua and Agawa for 9,000 years as part of their annual migrations. Winter hunting, spring maple sugaring, summer fishing and fall ricing constitute the annual cycle of recent history. During the fur-trade era, furs trapped inland during the winter were brought to Lake Superior camps in spring and hauled to distant trading posts. Having an HBC trading post next to their summer camps was a great improvement for the Indian people, giving them more time to catch and preserve fish, raise vegetables, pick berries and prepare for winter.

Company schooners and barges from Fort William and Michipicoten made several trips per year to serve the outposts. The schooner *Whitefish* picked up salt fish along with passengers and mail for delivery to the Sault. The barges from Michipicoten delivered trade goods and picked up furs for delivery to Michipicoten and thence to James Bay.

The winters were long, cold and lonely for company clerks isolated at the outposts. I can imagine that the first canoe coming down river and the first sail sighted on the horizon in spring were very welcome sights, indeed.

Out of the Fog

Fog is spooky, confusing and sometimes dangerous to your health. To be surrounded by thick fog on the lake is like being suspended in white space with no way to get your bearings.

On calm, overcast days in pea soup fog, there are no wind, waves or sun to orient you and your canoe or boat will travel in circles. You are lost but probably won't go very far.

Islands, rocks and reefs, normally familiar to you, will take on ghostly and strange shapes when you suddenly come on them in the fog. Sometimes you can imagine an island or tree line in the mist, but it's only an illusion not to be pursued. Being lost in the fog is a very lonely and frantic feeling.

Today's water travelers have compasses, charts, radar, depth sounders and global positioning systems that take some of the anxiety out of running in fog, but not all of it. It's still spooky traveling blind, guided only by hi-tech signals that are subject to hi-tech malfunctions. Even my simple magnetic compass doesn't always point north when I'm lost and trying to impose my will on it.

For more than 200 years, during the fur trade, voyageurs had neither compasses nor accurate charts to help them navigate the treacherous water route from Montreal toward the Canadian Northwest. On the big lakes of Huron and Superior their route was parallel with the shoreline, close enough to be able to scamper ashore to avoid inclement weather, yet far enough away to clear the many rocks and reefs in shallow waters. They spent many days stranded on shore because of high winds, heavy seas and dense fog.

But large inland lakes, like Saganaga in the boundary waters of Minnesota and Ontario, presented a different problem for voyageur canoes trying to navigate through the myriad of islands, rocks and reefs in thick fog. Even with experienced guides assigned to each brigade, it was difficult, on the clearest of days to maneuver through the complicated maze of islands to the next portage without compass or chart. Even the most experienced guides could get lost on Sag and have to hole up until the fog lifted.

I know of the relief one feels when the fog lifts and you find yourself in familiar surroundings. It's enough to make any voyageur want to sing again.

The compass, invented by the Chinese in about A.D. 900, has been in common use by explorers, surveyors and mapmakers since before Columbus. It's a mystery, to me, why the voyageurs didn't use them to help navigate their challenging routes.

Unloading at the Pic River – 1840

On my map the Pic River, the Black River and Swede River all share the same outlet into Lake Superior near Heron Bay. Independent fur traders used the Pic and the Black to access furs from Indian trappers on James Bay and Hudson Bay in the 1770s. Before 1800, the North West Company and the XY Company established trading posts at the mouth and were served by company ships like the *Otter* and *Perseverance* that periodically dropped off supplies and trade goods and picked up furs. It was also a welcome campsite for trade canoes en route between Sault Ste. Marie, Grand Portage and, after 1804, Fort William.

After 1821, and the Hudson's Bay Company takeover of the fur trade in Canada, things changed. The Lake Superior trade route declined severely as the Hudson's Bay Company preferred its traditional trade route using the Canadian waterways to its headquarters on Hudson Bay. Both the *Otter* and *Perseverance* were destroyed in the War of 1812, but after the war the *Recovery* and *Recovery II* resumed carrying the freight.

No longer the linchpin of Canadian fur trade, Fort William declined in activity and profit. Its importance was reduced to trading with local Indian people, a stopping-off place for company officials and dignitaries en route to trading posts at Fort Garry and the Northwest, and as a commercial fishery.

Hudson's Bay Company schooner *Whitefish* was built to serve what little fur trade survived and the new commercial fishing enterprise. Its ports of call included Fort William, the Pic, Michipicoten and Sault Ste. Marie. Its mission was to carry freight, passengers and mail along the east shore.

Freight included furs, fish, supplies and farm animals like pigs, horses and cows. The mouth of the Pic River is exposed to the entire stretch of Lake Superior to the southwest which precludes, in my opinion, the existence of wharves for ships to unload their cargoes. I believe they must have loaded and unloaded while anchored off shore, as my painting illustrates. Farm animals may have been pushed overboard to swim to shore or lowered in cargo nets or slings into waiting boats. All things considered, boat day must have been a rare but festive event for the isolated communities along the shore.

Schooner *Whitefish* at Michipicoten River

Michipicoten River, on Lake Superior's east shore, was used by woodland Indians as a trade route to James Bay on Hudson Bay long before fur traders Pierre Esprit Radisson and Médard Chouart des Groseilliers "discovered" it in 1660.

Fur traders from New France maintained a trading post at the mouth of the river for many years before the English took over Canada and the fur trade in 1763. Alexander Henry, the elder, was the first Englishman to occupy the post from 1767 to 1769. He left to seek his fortune in copper mining on Lake Superior.

Both the Hudson's Bay Company and the North West Company operated small trading posts across the river from each other, about one mile above the mouth, until the two companies merged in 1821.

After the merger, the Hudson's Bay Company directed almost all fur trade from the Northwest across Canada to Hudson Bay, the most efficient route to markets in England and Europe. With only furs from local Indian trappers to support it, Fort William rapidly declined in importance to the fur trade. But as Fort William lost importance, Fort Michipicoten gained, becoming the new hinge pin of Lake Superior's diminishing trade. Hudson's Bay Company's trading post at Michipicoten became the main depot serving secondary posts at Fort William, the Pic, Agawa, Sault Ste. Marie and James Bay.

Commercial fishing began at Hudson's Bay Company posts on Lake Superior in 1836 to supplement the dying fur trade. Company schooners like the *Whitefish* added whitefish, trout and sturgeon to their cargoes for Sault Ste. Marie, picking up kegs of salted fish at various fish stations along the way.

I assume loading and unloading the *Whitefish* was accomplished while anchored at the mouth of the Michipicoten River. Shallow water, shifting sand bars and strong river current prevented the large ship from navigating to the company wharf upstream. I'd guess that the schooner would fire a cannon announcing its unscheduled arrival. Fish kegs, mail and passengers finally arrived at the mouth from the trading post upriver to be loaded aboard the *Whitefish* at anchor.

H. Sivertson
© 2001

Swallow Arrives at Prince's Location

In 1846, a rich vein of silver ore stretching from Jarvis Bay to Spar Island was discovered on the Canadian north shore, 20 miles west of Thunder Bay. The major lode, deep under water, made it too difficult to mine efficiently with the technology of that era.

John Prince, owner of the claim, decided to mine the vein from both ends and sank a shaft on Spar Island and on the mainland at Jarvis Bay. He built the infrastructure needed to mine at both locations including, I would imagine, a warehouse, living quarters for miners, wharves at both locations to accommodate company work boats and schooners in the 40- to 80-ton class.

The schooner *Swallow,* one of the few sailing ships dragged by oxen over the portage at Sault Ste. Marie before the locks were opened in 1855, served the new mining communities and other settlements along the shore. She was large enough to carry seven passengers plus crew, one small fishing boat, one canoe and one larger boat.

In preparation for doing the painting, I visited Prince's location by boat and tried to imagine how it might have looked in 1848. It seemed obvious to me where the wharf was located. There is only one place, close to the mine shaft on Jarvis Bay, that had enough water and shelter from wind and waves yet was easily accessible from the big lake. It was just a matter, then, of researching the other elements and placing them where they belong.

This location was a traditional campsite for voyageurs and Indians for hundreds of years during the fur trade and before. By 1848, Ojibway people and Jesuit priests used this site on their frequent trips between Grand Portage, Pigeon River and Fort William.

John Prince mined with limited success at this location for two years before surrendering his dreams of riches to the impossible task of mining efficiently. The major lode of silver is still there at the bottom of the channel to tempt future prospectors.

Spring Journey to Pigeon River Mission – 1850

By 1835, Jesuit missionaries were beginning to return to Lake Superior's shores after being run off by Indian wars in the 1670s. Father Frederic Baraga was the first to arrive in 1835, as a passenger aboard the American Fur Company schooner *John Jacob Astor,* to establish his mission at La Pointe in the Apostle Islands. It took more than a decade for other priests to arrive to help Father Baraga bring Catholicism to Indians farther along the shore. Fathers Jean-Pierre Chone, Nicholas Fremiot, De Pooter, Francis Xavier Pierz, Dominique Chardon du Ranquet and Brother Frederick De Pooter arrived on the Canadian North Shore in the late 1840s.

A mission was established first at Pigeon River, then another near Fort William, with one priest serving both locations. Frequent trips were necessary to serve the local residents at both missions. The priests traveled in canoes and barges when the lake was free of ice and on snowshoes in winter over land and across ice, camping out along the way. The journey could take three days, exposing priests and company to life-threatening weather.

Indian families usually accompanied the priest, manning the oars in summer and breaking trail and pulling toboggans in winter. They served as guides and packhorses, helping the priests to accomplish their work.

Not all the trips were uncomfortable. I've spent many days in the Susie Islands area in balmy March weather that was totally enjoyable. I chose a similar day for the painting. Father du Ranquet describes that kind of day he experienced traveling from Fort William to Pigeon River in the spring of 1850, just before ice out. They traveled from shore trails to lake ice, sometimes in slush that clogged snowshoes, weighing them down and requiring frequent cleaning.

The Indian guide broke trail, his dog pulled the loaded toboggan and his family and the priest followed, enjoying a rare beautiful day while passing Finger Point in Pigeon Bay.

The Hudson Bay Trail to Grand Portage

Prehistoric people in the Lake Superior region followed game trails in pursuit of food, clothing and shelter. In a land barren of trees, the trails paralleled the rock ridges, which separated a multitude of lakes and rivers. Some of those trails still exist, centuries after the forest grew up around them.

Ojibway people probably used some of these well-worn ancient paths on their annual migrations to hunting, fishing, wild rice harvesting and maple sugar gathering camps. French, English and Scotch fur traders followed the same trails to find the Ojibway camps to collect furs and sell trade goods.

Sections of one of those trails can still be found meandering through the forest from Fort William to Grand Portage. Some old-timers say that the trail at one time ran all the way from Hudson Bay to Grand Portage. Some modern historians think that it was called the Hudson Bay Trail, named after the famed Hudson's Bay Company and used as a trade and mail route between Fort William and Grand Portage, up until the late-1800s.

Jesuit missionaries used the trail between Fort William, Pigeon Bay and Grand Portage to serve their missions at those locations year-round. In summer, they traveled by canoe. In winter, they traveled overland with snowshoes and toboggan, usually with local guides who lugged the luggage. The painting shows a guide helping a priest from the Fort William mission on the Hudson Bay Trail as it crests Mount Josephine on the way to Grand Portage.

In the late-1800s, local Ojibway residents used the trail to trade at the Parkerville Trading Post at the mouth of the Pigeon River.

Hot Lunch

North American Indians invented birch-bark canoes and toboggans long before European explorers arrived on the continent. The fur trade, as we know it, couldn't have happened without them. The tough, lightweight and versatile bark canoes and toboggans were instrumental in the exploration and settlement of North America's lake and river country. Canoes transported people, freight and mail in summer. Toboggans pulled by dogs or humans were the winter conveyance used for centuries in the frozen north by Indians, voyageurs, missionaries, trappers and mailmen.

French Canadian voyageurs modified the toboggan by adding a light frame with a backrest, enclosed with buffalo hide or canvas decorated with colorful designs, and called it a "cariole." Their tradition of equipping the sled dogs with pompoms and sleigh bells on their harnesses was popular well into the 20th century.

In the mid- to late-1800s, mail was delivered to new settlements along the north shore, to Canada and Isle Royale by mailmen and dog sleds (toboggans). They traveled on inland trails and ice-covered Lake Superior, enduring blizzards, bitter cold and the risk of breaking through thin ice on their long and lonely route.

Indian families, missionaries and trappers used frozen Lake Superior as their winter highway, too. Once the lake froze over, it was easier and shorter to mush along the shore than inland with all of its hills, ravines and rivers to cross. Winter travel on Lake Superior begin in the frigid month of January and lasted until the ice melted in early April.

By early March, mushers could expect a few relatively balmy days between blizzards and bitter cold. Those days of bright sun and no wind tempted the winter traveler to pull into a sheltered spot, build a fire, cook a hot lunch for himself and his dogs, then relax for a few minutes, basking in the warm sun, before mushing down the trail again.

H. SIVERTSON
©2007

A Village Named Skunk

Sweet harmonious melodies from John Eliasen's violin drifted through the quiet fishing village of Chicago Bay at sunset. Sentimental tunes from the old country accompanied the mewing of gulls perched atop fish houses tucked in along the bay, calmed the anxieties of the new immigrants, away from Norway for the first time.

John was the musician in the little fishing community, 20 miles east of Grand Marais, where he not only played for local dances but also walked, with violin tucked under his arm, to entertain folks in Tofte, Grand Marais and Grand Portage.

In 1888, the first immigrant settlers to arrive in Chicago Bay were Nels Eliasen and Ole Brunes aboard their homemade 26-foot fish boat. They fell in love with the beauty, built a house and promptly sent for families and relatives. Soon to follow were Johan Jacobsen and son, Bernt, Olaus Jacobsen, Emil and John Eliasen.

John Eliasen took it upon himself to add harbor improvement to his commercial fishing enterprise and dredged the main harbor of dangerous boulders, built an L-shaped boat slip in the gravel beach, then added a break-wall to protect it. The slip was large enough to accommodate several fishing boats, including his own. He then joined with his brother, Emil, Johan Jacobsen and Adolf Carlson to build a huge wharf, large enough to handle steamships like the *Hiram Dixon*.

When residents of the community found that the word Chicago was derived from the Ojibway word *shikag* meaning "skunk," they decided to change its name. Ole Brunes' mother suggested naming it "Hovland" after her father's estate in Norway. Maybe it was a stroke of genius or a touch of public relations savvy on her part. Her son, Ole, was about to enter the tourist business and inviting people to visit a village named "skunk" would not be productive, no matter how great the hotel or how good the sport fishing was.

Foolhardy Mission for the Census Taker – 1890

Anyone who knew anything about Lake Superior would have called the rowboat trip to Isle Royale by Burt Fessler and crew foolhardy. No one with any knowledge of Lake Superior's violent moods would have sent Burt with two helpers in an 18-foot rowboat loaded to the gunwales with camping gear and supplies, more than 200 miles on the world's most dangerous lake, just to take the census. It was especially foolish because the information that they went to collect was available from the bookkeeper at the Booth Fishery office in Duluth.

In May of 1890, Burt Fessler was appointed ichthyologist of the fisheries division of the 11th U.S. census. It was his first job after graduation from Indiana University with a bachelor's degree in ichthyology. His first assignment from his boss in faraway Washington, D.C., was to take the census and collect fishery data along Minnesota's north shore, from Duluth to Pigeon Point and Isle Royale.

The young man protested the assignment, informing his ignorant supervisor of the perils of such a trip and that the information wanted was easily obtained from the Booth Fish

Company that operated a freight boat, *Dixon,* on that same route twice weekly, making contact with every person along the route. But his boss insisted on doing it his way.

Burt and his two helpers set forth on July 31 in a rented 18-foot rowboat named *Bee,* and with two sets of oars and a small sail set off on the perilous journey. He reported encounters with storms, rain, cold, mosquitoes and a half-crazed fisherman. They finally made it to the Susie Islands where they flagged down the steamer *Dixon* at night using flaming birch-bark torches.

After a relatively uneventful trip on the *Dixon* to Thunder Bay and thence to Isle Royale, they once again took to their rowboat to complete their mission around the island. Burt records being treated with great hospitality by fishermen along the way. At Fisherman's Home they once more boarded the *Dixon* for the return trip to Duluth arriving on August 16.

Burt fell in love with the Arrowhead Region, settled in Duluth, became a lawyer, then a judge of the district court.

H. Sivertson
© 2003

Gathering Gull Eggs on Cloud Island

You don't hear much about anyone eating gull eggs any more. My father, who used to gather gull eggs for his mother on Isle Royale, says they tasted a little fishy when boiled or fried. Grandma used them mostly for baking bread.

Fur trader diaries record voyageurs raiding gull nests along their canoe routes, but they also used them in baking *galette,* bread made in a frying pan similar to bannock. John H. Malone, lighthouse keeper on Menagerie Island on Isle Royale from 1878 to 1893, recorded 1,478 gull eggs gathered in the spring of 1886. He didn't leave us any recipes, but I'd guess he fried and boiled a few besides using them in baked goods.

Dad had a system for separating mother gulls from their freshest eggs, those without chicks forming inside. On the first day, he rowed three miles to Gull Rock and drew an X with a crayon on every egg in the nests. The next day he simply took the eggs without an X. It was dangerous work, fighting angry mother gulls with one hand while stealing their eggs with the other.

Although I haven't found evidence that Indian people gathered gull eggs every spring, I assume they also would make use of the nutritious resource. Cloud Island near McKellar's Point has been a gull rookery for many generations and a good place to gather eggs, if you're so inclined.

The painting shows an Ojibway family collecting eggs on Cloud Island in the mid-1800s. The schooner sailing by could be delivering mail, supplies and passengers to the silver mine at Prince's location at Jarvis Bay or the Hudson's Bay Company Trading Post at Fort William.

First Mail Boat in Spring

Travel for the isolated settlers along the north shore in early spring was difficult if not impossible. Snow in the woods was melting, turning dog sled trails to slush, exposing large areas of mud and turning frozen rivers to exploding cascades of water and ice overflowing their banks. Lake ice melted next to shore and pockets of water lay on top of the ice fields eating away at the once-safe ice beneath it.

Mail delivery under those conditions was futile for carriers and frustrating for those waiting. Settlers along the shore, fur traders and Jesuit priests from Fort William and Pigeon Bay, silver miners at Silver Islet and copper miners on Isle Royale all waited anxiously for mail during that period when neither dog teams nor sail boats could operate.

In the unusually warm winter of 1875, two carriers on their way from Pigeon Bay to Isle Royale misjudged ice conditions and lost their lives. Mine owners, frustrated by lack of communication with the mine superintendent on Isle Royale, consulted a spiritual medium who finally made contact with the super and reported everything was hunky-dory at the mine, but no details made it through.

It's no wonder, then, when lake ice finally broke up, that survivors of the long, cold, lonely winter turned their eyes to scan the horizon for the first sails of spring. Spirits must have soared when the first mail boat sailed or rowed up to their landing with news and packages from home.

The first mail boat in spring would have sailed through islands and past shorelines still covered in ice. The crew maneuvered carefully among the ice floes still drifting with the wind.

The north shore mailmen's creed should include: "Neither thin ice, raging rivers, mountainous seas, wolves, moose, etc. … can keep these couriers from their appointed rounds." (Or something like that.)

H. Siverson
© 2002

When Mail Boats Meet

After the Civil War, north shore communities began to grow, requiring additional mail-carrying capacity. An influx of immigrants to fish and log, plus the discovery of silver at Silver Islet in Canada and the second era of copper mining on Isle Royale, made increased mail service necessary.

No longer was the 18-foot rowboat that served early residents scattered from Duluth to Pigeon Bay and Isle Royale capable of handling the growing demand for mail. Up until the 1880s, Canadians at Fort William, Prince Arthur's Landing and Silver Islet received mail from eastern Canada via Duluth, Minnesota.

A larger mail boat, needed to handle the mail for Canada, was added in 1873. It became the express mail boat, stopping only at Duluth and Canada once each week. The 18-foot rowboat continued its biweekly trips, stopping at every settlement and fish house from Duluth to Pigeon Bay.

It's hard for me to believe that the "express" mailman and the "local" mail carrier wouldn't stop to chat and compare notes when their routes crossed and weather permitted. Shop talk, weather, gossip, mineral finds, fishing success, large ships sighted and the multitude of languages they needed to understand from the new immigrants were probable topics of conversation.

Norskes, Swedes, Finns, Danes, Swiss, Irish, Germans, Scots, French and Chippewa all needed to communicate with the postmen along the shore.

Jack Scott, John Beargrease, John Morrison, Antoine Mashowah, Captains Holmgren, Peterson and Albert Weiland were probable skippers on the express schooners. J.W. Owen, Robert McLean, Chief Beargrease (father), George Ward, Joseph Montferrand and Louis Plante were among the famous mail carriers that rowed 18-foot boats along one of the most dangerous mail routes in the world.

Boat Days

Imagine yourself, like an eagle, overlooking Minnesota's Grand Marais Harbor from 1800 to 1900. What strange and interesting events would you witness in just 100 years?

Of course, you'd watch the comings and goings of the Ojibway people, just as they'd done for the previous 200 years or so, in small bark canoes or on snowshoes. Then, one day in 1803 you'd be surprised at the appearance of your first decked-over sailing ship, maybe the *Otter* or *Perseverance* from the North West Company trading post at Grand Portage, ducking into the harbor for protection during a storm.

After watching various vessels sneaking in and out of the harbor during the War of 1812, you'd witness the building of a small trading post on the beach by the American Fur Company in 1823, the same year Lieutenant Henry Bayfield of the British Admiralty may have anchored the *Recovery* in the harbor while surveying Lake Superior.

By 1835, American Fur Company ships *John Jacob Astor* and *William Brewster* were welcomed heartily by lonely company fishermen, as they unloaded supplies and picked up barrels of salt fish from the new fishery.

Small schooners like the *Swallow, Uncle Tom, Fur Trader* and *Algonquin* were enthusiastically greeted by small groups of prospectors and settlers at isolated ports, like Grand Marais, along the shore. After 1855, larger smoke-belching side-wheelers and propellers followed, bringing supplies and immigrants.

You'd watch a few prospectors and commercial fishermen linger on until the Civil War, when they left to do their duty. The town didn't come alive again until after the war when a few veterans and others settled in, seeking peace and quiet and possible riches.

In 1875, you saw the ice-covered schooner *Stranger* disappear forever in the frost smoke that hovered over the freezing lake. The tug *T.H. Camp* was welcomed on its infrequent trips hauling freight. Rowboats and sled dog teams delivered mail until the Booth Fishery started running the *Hiram Dixon* on a regular schedule hauling mail, freight and passengers. Finally, a boat day townspeople could depend on.

In just those 100 years, you witnessed the rise and fall of the fur trade era, the evolution of vessels from small bark canoes to wooden sailing ships to huge steel propeller-driven steamships. You watched as miners' dreams faded, majestic white pines were logged off, commercial fishing expanded, a town was built and breakwalls and lighthouses erected, tourism via steamships grew and Boat Day was celebrated whenever a ship entered the harbor.

Fishing Camp at Todd Harbor, Isle Royale – Circa 1900

Todd Harbor was probably one of the most popular locations on Isle Royale for prehistoric people and others that followed. Located about halfway down the north side of the island, it was the closest harbor of protection for people crossing from the Canadian mainland. The ancient peoples came to mine copper, fish, hunt, trap, make maple syrup and pick berries. A string of small islands protects the harbor from Lake Superior's storms, making it a natural harbor of refuge.

Copper eventually attracted the Pittsburg and Isle Royale Mining Company with Hugh McCullough as manager, who may have constructed some of the buildings on the mine site. The mine was productive for only six years, ending in 1853, after which McCullough turned to commercial fishing from the same location. I assume that most of his catch was sold to mining companies around Isle Royale. McCullough also owned and operated trading posts at Pigeon Bay and in the Boundary Waters between Canada and the United States.

Scandinavian immigrants were the next to fish at Todd Harbor and moved into the old McCullough location next to the abandoned copper mine. Fishing was excellent at Todd Harbor, but the fishermen were off the modern shipping lane and had to haul their catch many miles to Belle Isle to rendezvous with the *Hiram Dixon, America* or *Winyah* for shipment to market. The fishing station at Todd was finally abandoned due to the inconvenience of shipping their product.

For more than 5,000 years, families enjoyed the protection of Todd Harbor on mostly a seasonal basis. I assume the children of Ojibway, mining and fishing families played on the same beach while their parents harvested the adjacent resources for their survival.

Chippewa Harbor Settlement – Circa 1900

Whenever I turn my boat off the cold waters of Lake Superior into the warm sheltered fjord of Isle Royale's Chippewa Harbor, I think of Dorothy Simonson's first impression of the jewel-like harbor: "From where I'm sitting, I can look across 300 feet of clear turquoise water sparkling in the autumn sun, at a sheer rocky cliff, peopled with slim spires of evergreens. This is truly Isle Royale the beautiful." Dorothy was a schoolteacher and was accustomed to using poetic words to describe her feelings.

I'm sure the earthy Scandinavian immigrant commercial fishermen who arrived at Chippewa Harbor in the late 1800s felt the same way about the perfect harbor that provided perfect shelter next to one of the finest fishing grounds on Lake Superior. Their hymns of praise may have included: "Ya … it's OK, I guess. Kinda reminds me of the old country and I don't have to sail far to the fishing."

Among the first Scandinavians to settle and fish out of Chippewa Harbor were Godfrey Vodrey, Otto Olsen, Sam Johnson and Holgar Johnson and their families. They came to fish lake trout, whitefish and herring on a seasonal basis, returning to the mainland in winter. Some families like the Holgar Johnsons wintered-over on Isle Royale during the worst Depression years in the 1930s. Holgar hired Dorothy Simonson to teach his children on Isle Royale during the winter of 1932 and '33.

They built good, solid mackinaw schooners to fish from, but their "temporary, seasonal homes" were slapped together to make do for just one more season. However, they kept returning to the beautiful harbor year after year, still patching their shacks that sometime through the years became their homes, community and culture. "Ya … Isle Royale's the only place for me. … They'll have to take me outta here in a box … you bet."

Port Coldwell

The Ontario north shore of Lake Superior attracted the famed Canadian Group of Seven artists to its dramatically rugged and beautiful shores in the 1920s. Small communities of miners, loggers, railroad workers and commercial fishermen were tucked into the many harbors of the ragged coastline.

Photos of thriving Canadian fishing communities from the early 1900s look like they may have come from my family's photo album. Boats, docks, people, houses and freight ships are remarkably similar to those at Isle Royale and along the north shore. Settlements like Mamainse Harbour, Lizard Islands, Gargantua Harbour, Brule Harbour, Michipicoten Island, Nipigon, Rossport, Jackfish Bay and Port Coldwell are a few of the villages scattered along the coast that relied on commercial fishing until the sea lamprey and rainbow smelt decimated lake trout populations and reduced thriving communities to ghost towns.

Port Coldwell was just one of several coastal towns that was shut down and abandoned after the trout were gone. In the 1880s, Port Coldwell was adjacent to good fishing grounds that supported a community of fishing families. It was also a supply depot for the building of the new Montreal to Winnipeg leg of the Canadian Pacific Railway. Each summer, locals set up a tent village during the blueberry picking season. The arrival of the newly constructed Highway 17 in 1960 coincided with the closing of the village and the railroad depot. Automobiles can now whiz past without being aware of one of the most dramatic, scenic and historic places on the entire Lake Superior shoreline.

Lawren Harris and other artists from the Group of Seven traveled hundreds of miles on rail or steamship to paint the dramatic lighting, stark forms and glistening waters of Port Coldwell in her heyday. It's quite possible that they arrived on a freight boat similar to the one in the painting. Theirs was truly the golden age of art along the spectacular Canadian shore where colorful people led interesting and productive lives in quaint, picturesque settlements.

Blueberries

On my way to beachcombing in the Susie Islands, I found a secluded beach near Pigeon Point that was sheltered from all but the stormiest weather. I eased my boat onto the gravel beach and tied it to a log to keep it from wandering off. After casually inspecting the beach for artifacts or interesting driftwood, I climbed the gradual slope behind the beach and found a large patch of ripe blueberries that covered the hillside.

After eating my fill, I loaded my bailing can with the juicy berries for muffins and pancakes back home.

It was a beautiful, dead calm day, a rare opportunity on Lake Superior to relax and enjoy the beach without fear of changing weather that could force me to leave. While picking at the stones near the water's edge, I thought of other cultures that probably picked berries on the same hill and camped on the same beach, centuries before I discovered them.

I imagined an Ojibway family picking blueberries during summer encampment on the shore. (It was the women's and children's job to pick berries while the men probably did more important things like smoking and talking around the fire.)

The beach was full of flat stones that I skipped across the water and I imagined kids doing the same thing for hundreds of years while mothers nagged them to quit fooling around and start picking. Don't eat them! Fill the makuks first! We must live on berries next winter. By springtime you'll be sorry you were so lazy.

Summer must have been a good time for Ojibway families who got together on the shore of Lake Superior to catch and preserve fish, raise potatoes, pick and preserve berries. Soon, they headed inland to harvest the wild rice lakes. Then the band broke up and families migrated to their cold, isolated hunting grounds.

If they found enough game and if they preserved enough fish, potatoes, wild rice, maple sugar and berries to make it through the winter, then they'd once again return to the big lake to celebrate survival. And if they were lucky, they would return to this ideal cove and a hillside full of blueberries.

H. Sivertson
©2001

Island Retreat

I've got a thing about islands. They're quite often the subjects of my paintings. I've never consulted a specialist about my obsession, but it could be because my roots are on Isle Royale where my family lived for three generations until they were forced to leave so the government could create a playground for "the benefit of the greater good." It's hard to replace island life by living somewhere else, but I continue the search.

By now, after more than 30 years of looking, my 20-foot boat almost knows its own way around the islands of western Lake Superior. In the process, beachcombing has become a hobby in my search for the perfect island retreat. Interesting driftwood and artifacts from past cultures catch my eye, but I leave them where I find them. They're more at home on the beach than in my living room.

Some islands have a history of early occupation by prehistoric people. Archaeologists have found arrowheads and pottery shards at natural campsites. Woodland Indians used islands as fishing camps, hunting, berry picking and as a refuge from enemy tribes. The Hudson's Bay Company used islands with natural harbors for seasonal commercial fishing camps that were eventually re-occupied by Metis, then Scandinavian immigrant fishermen.

I'm especially attracted to islands that are ideal for at least semi-subsistence living. A sheltered harbor for fish house and dock, a home site and garden area, things that my family lost on Isle Royale, seem the most interesting to me. The island in my painting is such a place. I invented the fish house, dock and fisherman rowing home in his skiff to complete the ideal place.

But even more than a sentimental connection with my roots, islands are places of refuge from the constant noise and demands of others. They're ideal places for long-term meditation where, if you stay long enough, you can finally hear your own voice instead of the loud persistent babble of others.

Henry David Thoreau had his cabin on Walden Pond. The prophets had the desert. Moses had Mount Sinai. For me, the islands of western Lake Superior provide a place of solitude and meditation.

Dead Reckoning

'Ivasen't lost, I just didn't know vhere vas I," was the answer to the Norwegian fishermen standing on Booth Dock at Washington Harbor. Martin Christiansen had just navigated the steamship *Winyah* through more than 100 miles of dense fog around Isle Royale, guiding his 118-foot freight boat safely through hundreds of islands, rocks and reefs on his perilous rounds without mishap. He had no modern high-tech electronic instruments like radar, depth sounders or global positioning systems to help him.

He had only a compass and watch and the knowledge of how fast his ship traveled, plus experience, intuition, ears, eyes and nose to guide him. His courses around the island were drawn on his lake chart in the pilothouse and included compass directions and running times between various points along the way. The variables like wind and current were intuitively adjusted for by the seat-of-the-pants method. This system of navigation, called dead reckoning, has been used for hundreds of years and is still the fallback system used by wise captains who also use modern electronic gadgets subject to malfunctioning.

Martin Christiansen, running in dense fog, made his turn around Rainbow Point, adjusted his course for Booth Island, ran out his time, but could barely see the bow of his ship let alone any landmarks. He slowed the engine to a crawl, so he wouldn't crash into the islands that surrounded him, and gave three toots on his steam whistle. The fishermen on Booth Dock anticipated the signal and immediately answered by pounding a hammer on an empty gas barrel, guiding the *Winyah* the last 100 yards to the dock. Martin could barely see the fishermen who were handling his lines and giving him the raspberries about being "lost."

Commercial fishermen used the dead reckoning method of navigation when running between gangs of nets or hook lines or returning home in fog. Their charts were in their heads. Courses and times memorized. Intuition, plus noses, ears and eyes were a major part of the system. They could smell land, hear gulls and birds and recognize landfalls. Many "lost" boats were guided home by the bell-like tones of hammers hitting gas barrels.

Sam and Helpers Homeward Bound

If there had been child labor laws in the early 1900s, my grandfather would have spent most of his life in prison. Sam wasn't a cruel man. It was just the way things were. It was the way he and all his ancestors were raised. When kids reached 8 or 12 years old, they were put to useful purpose.

Every morning, just before daybreak, my father and one of his two sisters, Myrtle or Bertha, were rousted from their warm beds to go on the cold lake with their father, Sam, to row the 26-foot mackinaw fishing schooner to the nets. A fire was lit in the wood stove where the sleepy-eyed children tried to stay warm while struggling into their warmest clothes, some still wet from yesterday.

The house was just warming up when they finished breakfast and shuffled down the path to the boat, waiting by the dock still slippery with frost. A morning breeze, rising with the sun, would perhaps fill the sails on the 5-mile run to the nets. The kids pulled on their supposedly waterproof oilskins and picked their favorite places on the boat, where they huddled out of the wind but where the sun would reach them with warming rays.

Dad and Myrtle, each wielding a heavy 9-foot oar, rowed the boat while Sam lifted and reset the nets, shouting orders, in Norwegian, past the stem of his ever present pipe to "rew up" (against the current) or "rew down" (with the current) to keep the boat precisely where he wanted it. The exercise and sun soon warmed them enough to stimulate them to horseplay.

As long as Sam's back was to them, they could tease, giggle, swat at water bugs with their oars and splash each other with water, all the while staying tuned to Sam's gruff orders. Finally by mid-afternoon, the last buoy was dropped over the side, sails were hoisted and the boat turned homeward.

The prevailing southwest wind filled the sails, allowing the kids to ship oars and rest. Sailing before the wind down Grace Harbor gave their tired, sometimes seasick, bodies and blistered and bloodied hands a chance to heal and catch some sleep before landing and helping with shore work and chores until dark.

Dad, wistfully, complained to me in his later years that he couldn't remember ever having had a chance to play when he was a kid growing up on Isle Royale.

Towing Pond Net Stakes to Isle Royale

It was a long, cold night towing pond net stakes across Lake Superior from Grand Portage to Isle Royale. We barely made headway dragging too many 20- to 25-foot logs or stakes with a too-small and underpowered boat in pitch black of night. I introduced moonlight in the painting to show what was happening.

In 1943, Sivertson Brothers decided to re-introduce pond (or pound) net fishing at Isle Royale to catch herring and whitefish the way they used to on the island – and still do on the south shore of Lake Superior.

Pond nets and fly traps are similar in that both use the principle of leading and confusing their victims into a maze that directs them to an end chamber where they cannot find their way out. Pond nets have heavily tarred nets, hung from a series of stakes. The fish are led into a maze going to the "pot" or live trap where they're held alive until fishermen empty the pot each day. Twenty- to 25-foot-long stakes are driven into the bottom of the lake using a pile driver mounted on a barge. When the correct pattern of stakes is set, the tarred net is hung on the poles.

Cutting trees for stakes was forbidden by park service regulation so the tall, straight, slender jack pines had to be cut on the Minnesota shore and delivered to Grand Portage Bay. It was my job to partially debark the poles before launching them for the tow. We hoped that the grinding and jostling together during the tow would finish the job.

Once the net is in place, pond net fishing is an easy, efficient and ecologically sound method of fishing. All fish are alive when the net is lifted, which means fresher fish in the market. Any unwanted species are returned, alive, to the lake.

The best fishing grounds for pond nets on Isle Royale were exposed to the lake's wrath, which tore up the nets too often. After a few years, pond net fishing, with limited success, proved once again to be too inefficient for the waters around Isle Royale.

H. SIVERTSON
© 2001

Green Island Fishery

Today, there's little left on Green Island to give evidence of the small group of fisher folk who lived there years ago. Except for a dilapidated rock crib that used to support a dock and fish house and a couple of grown-over clearings that marked building sites, the small island remains silent, keeping its secrets to itself.

The inhabitants of the island left no diaries or records of what their lives were like, sequestered on the lonely little island, and tucked into the northeast corner of Todd Harbor on Isle Royale. What did they do for excitement or entertainment to give them relief from the hard work and monotony of harvesting fish from Lake Superior?

I camped on Green Island several years ago and was taken by the extraordinary beauty and peaceful solitude of the place. That was entertaining enough for me, for a while. But a person gets used to perfection and after a time it becomes boring. While sitting on a rocky outcrop overlooking Todd Harbor and its islands gazing toward the Canadian shore, I realized that there were other fish camps within just a few miles of Green Island that made up a community of people who occasionally got together for social events, relieving the boredom.

For bright lights and dancing, the fancy Belle Isle Resort lured them down the Amygdaloid Channel just an hour and a few drams of whiskey away. The resort provided entertainment for its fashionable guests and island folks in the area. Several island fishermen courted, then married, employees from resorts, lodges and hotels around Isle Royale.

Large cruise ships and mail and freight boats offered more color and excitement to isolated fishermen and families. Palatial cruise ships like the *North American, South American, Huronic* and *Noronic* made frequent stops at Isle Royale bringing thousands of visitors to the island.

Once in a while a ship would crash and sink in island waters, providing a diversion for island folks. The 250-foot Canadian steamship *Kamloops* stranded then sank at 12 O'clock Point, just one-half mile from Green Island on December 7, 1927. If the residents of Green Island had delayed their departure for the season just a few days, they would have witnessed the tragic event and been in position to rescue seven of the crew who were found frozen on the beach in a makeshift lean-to the following spring. One man had a Life Saver candy still clutched in his hand.

All things considered, Green Island was as close to paradise for a fishing camp as I'll ever find again.

The *Winyah* at Edisen's Fishery

Captain Martin Christiansen had to maneuver the steamship *Winyah* through several reefs to finally land at Pete Edisen's dock at Rock Harbor, one of the few private docks with deep enough water to accommodate the 118-foot freighter from Duluth. She announced her impending arrival with a couple of blasts from her steam whistle about 1 mile from the dock, enough warning for the fishermen to get their boxes and kegs of fish out on the dock ready for loading.

The women had time to slip into something less dowdy in which to greet the boat and its fashionable tourist passengers who lined the bow rail to watch as fish were loaded after empty boxes, kegs, salt, ice and gasoline barrels were unloaded.

The scruffy half-shaven men scurrying about in fish clothes and rubber knee boots shouting to each other in thick Norwegian accents and their peasant-appearing women, with fresh rouge and bright head scarves, aroused the curiosity of the sophisticated passengers looking down from the ship's railing at the flurry of activity. It was not uncommon for a passenger to inquire of someone on the dock whether they could read or write. The mail passing back and forth between the women and the ship's mate should, of course, have been a clue.

But their rough appearance belied the truth about the real island folks. Among those fishermen on the docks around Isle Royale were folks of all walks of life, in the old country and the new. One strange looking little guy had been the chief accountant for a major lumber company in Norway. Several were ex-sailors and officers in the Norwegian Merchant Marine. Two fishermen, of neater appearance, were members of the Duluth Board of Trade. Two brothers owned and operated their own fish company, transportation company, boat dealership, engine dealership and marine equipment company in Duluth, all accomplished simultaneously and successfully with only eighth grade educations. Several fishermen would habitually migrate to the bowery after the fall fishing was over, then to the county work farm for the winter.

From the deck of the *Winyah,* they all looked the same, working side by side to get the job done on Boat Day.

Racing the Squall

Pete glanced over his shoulder to see how fast the squall was gaining on him as he sped for home at 9 miles per hour. In a lifetime of commercial fishing on Isle Royale, Pete had been caught in many squalls and survived. A few years earlier, while guiding a sport fishing party off Blake's Point on the extreme northeast end of Isle Royale, he saw another squall coming on fast, which produced winds up to 100 miles per hour. They barely got their hooks in and took cover behind Blake's Point before large trees, uprooted by the wind, flew over their boat into Merritt Lane.

If Pete hadn't reached the protection of Blake's Point in the nick of time, he wouldn't have lived to race this squall home. The ominous black clouds scudding over the lake at more than 30 miles an hour were gaining on him. Pete reached over to the engine box and pulled the throttle out to high speed, which was about 11 miles per hour. If this squall had caught him while he was farther out on the lake lifting nets, he would have tied his boat to the anchor buoy and waited it out. It could be just another storm but, then again, it could be a violent storm with disastrous results. He had no choice now but to run for the sheltered cove, try to get his boat tied up at the dock and watch the squall roar by from the fish house door.

Seafaring people had many proverbs, in addition to their barometers, to help forecast the weather. "Red sky in the morning, sailors take warning, red sky at night, sailors delight." "A backing wind says storms are nigh, but a veering wind will clear the sky." "Rainbow to windward, foul fall the day, rainbow to leeward, rain runs away." "A halo around the sun indicates the approach of a storm within three days, from the side which is the most brilliant." "Sound traveling far and wide, a stormy day does like betide."

Island folks had one saying that was simpler and easier to remember: "When you hear thunder or see lightning, get off the lake."

Beach Net Fishing

The shallow waters around islands, beaches and sheltered coves were sort of reserved for old retired fishermen or for the young kids just starting out. They could make a few dollars to supplement Social Security or to spend on clothes and stuff when going back to school.

Serious fishermen, supporting families, had to go where the big fish were plentiful, which usually meant far away and down deep. Hook line fishing and deep-water net fishing required big boats and heavy-duty equipment to do the job. A strong body that could do the heavy lifting and withstand the rigors of daily encounters with the big, open lake was also necessary.

Grandpa Sam Sivertson set his nets in shallow water in sheltered coves that produced a few fish without the necessity of coping with the lake's extreme moods. All he needed was his 16-foot rowboat, a 2½ horsepower outboard motor and Grandma or one of his grandchildren to row along the nets. Dad informed me when it was my turn to help Grandpa and I knew I was in for a long day with the "old man."

Grandpa and I never communicated other than his two-word commands to direct my rowing or reprimands for my lack of manners. On the lake, he gave gruff orders to: "Rew up" (against the current), "Rew down" (with the current) and "Go ahead and rew backwards." At home it was: "Take your cap off, sit down and be quiet." And "Don't touch my radio." His grandchildren knew there was music somewhere in that box with knobs, not just weather reports, news and static.

Sam was a scrawny, rawboned man who, when standing precariously balanced on the tiny stern seat of the boat, hunched over, lifting nets, resembled a question mark with a pipe. I had to row with slow, steady strokes. Any sudden movement would toss Grandpa into the lake and I was too small to pull him back into the boat.

Now, I regret not getting to know him better. All I know about him I heard from others. He was a cabin boy on a Norwegian sailing ship that traded around the world. He fished with his father in the fjords of Norway. He sang in the church choir in the old country and he proclaimed himself "king of the vest end" in West Duluth's bowery district.

Grandpa's nets were set in beautiful locations amongst the islands, close to gorgeous beaches strewn with driftwood, pretty stones and interesting artifacts. Sam didn't give me much conversation, but he did introduce me to a lot of places that I'll always love.

Wintering Over on Isle Royale

Compared to the rest of the country during the Depression and dust bowl years of the 1930s, Isle Royale residents survived well. They stocked up with provisions before the last freight boat left in the fall. Together with garden vegetables and wild berries, canned in the summer, and fish and moose available just out the front door, they lived quite well. If being isolated on an island all winter didn't bother them, it was a relatively good place to wait out the bad times, depending on your point of view, of course.

Fisherman Pete Edisen: "The finest thing a man can do is to winter over on Isle Royale. It's beautiful!"

School teacher Dorothy Simonson: "It's November 22, 1932, and for the first time we realized we were indeed isolated on this block of snow and ice with its threatening fir-crowned cliffs and howling wolves, its frozen stars and frost moon surrounded by nothing but a seething turbulence that men call Lake Superior."

Fisherman Milford Johnson: "We shot a few moose, trapped some coyotes and cut wood and cut wood and cut wood to heat our drafty lighthouse."

Fisherman John Skadberg: "What I remember most is my fishing partner who brought over 500 pounds of sugar in the fall. He made beer and stayed drunk all winter."

To avoid the high cost of mainland living during the Depression, several people wintered over on the island. John Skadberg and Otto Olson at Hay Bay. The Holgar Johnson Family and his children's schoolteacher, Dorothy Simonson, were at Chippewa Harbor. Milford and Arnold Johnson, Jack Bangsund, Pete Edisen at Rock Harbor were among those who sought refuge on Isle Royale.

They survived by fishing, hunting, trapping, cutting wood and visiting each other. They traveled by boat, snowshoes and skates, 15 to 20 miles just to visit and escape the loneliness.

Pete Edisen was skating down Rock Harbor to visit the winter caretaker at the Rock Harbor Lodge, six and a half miles away, when he saw a moose trying to cross over to Mott Island on glare ice. Pete thought, since he was going so fast on that glare ice, the moose figured it would try it, too. By gosh, when the moose got out on that slick surface, its feet went out and its chin hit the ice.

Compared to howling dust storms, bread lines and soup kitchens the rest of the country experienced, wintering over on Isle Royale was a walk in the park.

Free Ice

In the early days, before refrigeration, commercial fishermen usually salted down the fish they caught for market, in kegs and barrels. Fish, properly preserved in salt brine, lasted for many months. Sometimes fish were preserved by drying or freezing outdoors, but success depended on consistent weather conditions.

With the advent of faster freight boats making more frequent trips, and trucks and trains equipped with refrigeration, fish could be shipped fresh to distant markets. Lake trout, whitefish and herring – constantly packed in ice from the moment they're caught until the moment they're sold – could be eaten "fresh" by consumers all across the country.

But ice was expensive for fishermen in remote areas like Isle Royale. They had to buy manufactured ice in 200-pound blocks from commercial ice companies in Duluth. No matter how much those blocks shrunk en route, they were billed for the entire 200 pounds. By the time the ice reached the fishermen on the freight boat, it weighed about 150 pounds or less. Fishermen buried the ice under sawdust in icehouses. When they finally used it, the precious blocks weighed less than 75 pounds.

But free ice was available on the island, for those who arrived at Isle Royale early enough in the spring. Clear blue ice, created by wave action in winter, still covered the rocks on the north, shaded side of islands and the mainland and was available free to the fishermen willing to harvest it. With ice chisels, axes and tongs they could chop it loose from the rocks, then hoist the valuable chunks into the boat for delivery to the icehouse. Covered thick with sawdust, shore ice would last until midsummer, after which they had to order the expensive stuff from the ice companies.

Fishermen living near sheltered coves and bays, which remained frozen over after ice on the big lake was gone, cut some lake ice. Portable ice cube machines were finally available at the very end of the commercial fishing era on Isle Royale. But that wasn't free ice.

The Inevitable Race Home Through Middle Island Passage – Circa 1936

People made their own fun in the small isolated communities around Isle Royale. At Rock Harbor, Milford and Arnold Johnson were especially good at it. Born and raised in the commercial fishing family of Mike and Nellie Johnson, the brothers were good friends who competed in everything they did. They tried to catch more fish, work faster, play harder and, of course, race their boats at every opportunity.

Both had helped their father fish since they were old enough to reach the rim of a salt fish barrel. By 8 years old they were expected to help out on the lake. Both boys, after watching a drunken hired man drive shingle nails into his leg, had to try it for themselves. It wasn't until they suffered a lot of pain that they found out about the wooden leg. As a young man, Milford rode a moose swimming in Lake Ritchie to win a $50 bet from Dr. Frank Oastler.

Milford and Arnold fished together as a team for a number of years, married about the same time and both raised their growing families in the abandoned Rock Harbor Lighthouse. Myrtle had four children at the lighthouse and Olga had two. Milford was obviously winning that race.

They decided to split up the fishing partnership after awhile. Each brother bought his own boat and rigging. Milford bought the 24-foot *Seagull* powered by a gray marine engine. Arnold bought the *Belle* with a Scripps engine. The *Seagull* had speed, about 10 mph. The *Belle* had more power.

Both brothers had similar rigs, fished in the same area and worked at about the same speed, which leaves the boat race home through the Middle Island Passage to determine the winner. Every day, when the children at the lighthouse heard their fathers' engines, they'd run out on the rocks to watch the race and cheer on their fathers. Milford and the *Seagull* always won.

Of course, Milford's kids teased Ronny and Yvonne mercilessly. Ronny always countered by claiming his dad's boat was carrying more fish, slowing it down.

Ronny died just after I started painting the picture. As a memorial to him, I painted the *Belle* winning the race for the first time.

Going Visiting

She met her handsome Norwegian at a dance in town and he swept her off her feet. He was clean-cut, smelled of rose water and loved to laugh, dance and sing. She was young, sylph-like with sparkling eyes, smelled of lilacs and loved to laugh, dance and sing.

They got married. He took her to his homestead on the north shore where he introduced her to the life of a commercial fisherman's wife. She cooked, baked, canned, sewed, cleaned, washed clothes, tended a garden and livestock and raised children, all without the convenience of running water, indoor plumbing or electricity. Her only appliance was the huge wood-burning stove.

He worked hard all day on the lake. He smelled of salt brine, fish guts, pine pitch, boot socks and snoose. She became strong, hard muscled with frizzy hair, in need of a manicure and smelled of Hi-Lex, Pine Sol, fresh bread, kerosene and dirty diapers. By day's end, they were too tired to laugh, dance or sing or even wonder if they were still in love or not. Certainly no one thought to mention it.

But even a Norwegian immigrant fisherman knows his wife may need a break from the drudgery of pioneering.

There weren't many options to entertain each other at their isolated location along the shore, with the closest neighbors several miles away. Visiting friends from the old country was exciting for the whole family. Hiking miles of footpaths over rugged terrain, wearing their best finery, was out of the question. The easiest travel was by boat.

When the weather was perfect and nets had been tended, they scrubbed the fish boat, themselves and the kids. They loaded the boat with picnic baskets full of goodies, blankets, concertina or violin and maybe a precious bottle of whiskey to treat friends. He smelled of rose water and she of lilacs.

They were joyfully welcomed. After eating, they laughed, danced and sang. While the women chatted and cleaned up, the men sauntered to the boat for a dram or two and talked of fishing. When the weather dictated that it was time to leave, tears were shed as everyone hugged good-bye.

After they arrived back home, lanterns were lit, children tucked in and he almost said he loved her. She still smelled of lilacs and he like roses, with just a hint of snoose and whiskey.

Partners

Myrtle rowed her father Sam Sivertson's boat on the nets when she was a kid at Washington Harbor on Isle Royale. So, rowing her husband, Milford Johnson, on the nets wasn't a new experience. In fact, Myrtle could probably have handled the fishing rig by herself if she hadn't been busy raising six boys and one girl on the island.

Milford fished with his father, Mike, at Rock Harbor, 45 miles northeast of where Myrtle fished with her father, Sam, at Washington Harbor. Sometime in the 1920s, they started courting each other. Mel was a gallant suitor, running his fish boat the 45 miles to see her, then returning home by early morning in time to go on the nets. Their marriage in 1928 probably saved his life and his boat engine.

Myrtle and Mel shared the first few years of married life with his brother, Arnold, and sister-in-law, Olga, in the abandoned Rock Harbor Lighthouse. By the late 1930s, they moved to Star Island and, in the late 1940s, moved for the final time to Amygdaloid Island on the northeast end of Isle Royale.

Milford was one of the most productive fishermen on the island. He worked hard and played hard. Myrtle worked even harder but didn't have time to play. She led the typical pioneer woman's life, raising her children, doing all the household chores without benefit of electricity, running water or indoor plumbing, plus helping her husband on the lake and in the fish house.

By the time the kids were grown, lake trout fishing was petering out and Park Service regulations prohibited the next generation of fishermen from living on the island. The young people had to leave the island and find work on the mainland.

Mel was getting too old to go on the lake by himself. His boat was rotting out with no money to replace or even fix it. They couldn't afford a hired man, so Myrtle once again took her place in the boat next to Mel and together they caught enough fish to supplement Social Security.

Mel died on the island, was packed in ice and shipped to Two Harbors for burial. Myrtle followed shortly, putting an end to a lifelong, sometimes rocky, partnership, but they weathered every storm together.

Standoff at the Grace Island Raspberry Patch

Raspberries ripened toward mid-summer on Isle Royale and we all had our favorite patches to pick. Raspberries are easier to pick than blueberries. You can pick standing up and the berries are larger and fill the container faster. You can pick a patch clean one day and come back the next day and do the same thing.

Our family's favorite patch was on Grace Island in Washington Harbor. It was about a half-mile row to the little cove protected from the wind. We each carried an empty two-pound coffee can with a string attached so the can could hang from our necks leaving both hands free for picking. We kept a large bread dough-making pan in the boat to empty our full cans into.

In the center of the little island the raspberry bushes grew far above our heads as they reached for the light. We had to climb windfalls to reach the top branches where berries grew in clusters, almost like grapes.

If Mother heard me slip and fall off a high windfall and crash to the ground, she didn't inquire as to my well-being but screamed, "Did you spill any berries?"

Cow moose liked Grace Island for its good grazing and the protection from wolves that it offered to their calves. Cow moose can be quite dangerous when protecting their calves, so, if confronted, it would behoove one to have patience and hope that she wanders off to another part of the island once she is satisfied of your peaceful intentions.

Going Home After the Dance

The hard-working fisher folk on Isle Royale looked forward to the big dance and "Sänger fest" on the Fourth of July. Dowdy-looking women and grungy men metamorphosed into beautiful ladies and handsome gentlemen after a bath and dressing in clothes reserved for church, funerals and "the Fourth."

The entire community boarded freshly scrubbed fish boats for the trip to the dance at Singer Hotel, Washington Club, Caribou Island or wherever they could find room to accommodate ballroom dancing. They whirled about the dance floor effortlessly to waltzes, two steps, polkas and schottisches to spirited music from concertina, fiddle and sometimes piano. If my grandmother's dancing partner got too tired or tipsy to keep up with her, she'd put her strong arm around him, grab him by the back of his pants, lift and twirl with him around the floor, his feet never touching. It wasn't quite like Fred and Ginger, but close enough.

Island people loved to sing, too. One old fisherman carried a pitch pipe with him to keep everyone in tune.

Their lusty voices in four-part harmony echoed through the islands. Old country ballads and anthems brought tears to their eyes and shivers up their spines. Many had good choir training at church or singing chorales in the old country or Duluth. Even in old age, their voices were forceful enough to raise gulls off the water on the downbeat.

Singing continued above the drone of boat engines on the way home from the dance. If Uncle Gust was sober enough, his fairly middling renditions of operatic arias would bounce off the islands and hills, drowning out even the loudest engines.

With sleeping kids wrapped in blankets stuffed in the bow and adults still belting out sentimental and patriotic World War II songs in the stern, boats wound through islands and reefs toward home with only the moon and a billion stars to guide them.

Going to the Beach

He stepped out of the fish house, stood on the dock, scanned the sky and said, "Go tell your mother we're going to the beach for gravel." The boy turned and ran to the house with the news, picking up his Prince Albert tobacco can, now filled with angleworms, on his way back to the dock. By the time they shoved the skiff off the slide at the dock and rigged a tow line to the gas boat, the mother came down the trail with the baby under one arm and a picnic basket under the other. They threw a dozen burlap coffee sacks into the skiff and headed for the beach, two miles away.

It was that time of year to fill gravel sacks used as anchors for nets and hook lines. There's not a lot of time or opportunity for exciting entertainment on the island and they had to be ready for any occasion that offered a fun break in their busy lives. She'd been ready for days. The boy had dug the worms yesterday. There was always a chance, if the weather held after the sacks were filled, that his dad would allow him a few minutes to fish for speckled trout in the mouth of the creek next to the beach.

They anchored the gas boat off shore and rowed the short distance to the beach in the wooden skiff. They worked fast. The father shoveled gravel from the beach into the sacks held open by his son in the skiff. He filled the sacks to a weight he could barely lift, then tied the tops shut. They moved the skiff off the beach where it would continue to float while taking on more weight. The father kept an anxious eye on the weather. Dead calm was necessary to load the skiff and tow it back to the fish house.

The mother had spread a picnic lunch on a blanket on the beach and was beachcombing for agates, driftwood and possibly some ripe raspberries. Speckle trout were jumping in the creek, but by the time the coffee sacks were full, the leaves started trembling from a breeze out of the southwest. The gravel sacks weighed the skiff down to where it started leaking through the side seams.

The son sensed the weather change. Just a glance from his father told him that the picnic was over. They put the picnic basket and baby into the skiff and shoved off for the gas boat. They'd eat lunch on the way home, towing a skiff rapidly taking on water against a sea rising with the wind. Maybe next year.

Rowing the Laundry to Grandma's

Mother felt fortunate to have washdays when she could use Grandma's automatic washing machine to do her mountains of laundry. Dad had invented a wash machine for mother using an outboard motor and a large barrel, but it needed some "fine tuning" before he would dare starting it up again. Grandma's professionally designed and manufactured apparatus looked simple enough, using an agitator in a washtub powered by a single cylinder air-cooled gasoline engine driving a series of belts to agitate the agitator. The kick-starter was foot-powered, somewhat like a motorcycle. The wringer still had to be cranked by hand.

All mother had to do was load her washtubs and wicker baskets full of dirty clothes onto the wheelbarrow and, with two kids in tow, push it down the rock-strewn path to the skiff by the dock. She piled laundry and kids into the boat and rowed it one-half mile to Grandma's place, where she loaded Grandpa's wheelbarrow with her laundry and pushed it up his rocky path to Grandma's house and the wonderful machine that was supposed to "take the work out of wash day."

After hauling what seemed to be a hundred pails of water from the lake to the washtubs and copper boilers on the wood stove, she confronted the cantankerous, temperamental shin-barking engine. She stomped on the crank until her leg cramped up, then switched to the other leg. Finally, after changing and adjusting half a dozen spark plugs taken from a coffee can next to the engine, it coughed, sputtered and, in a cloud of blue smoke, it started.

She dumped clothes, hot water and soap into the agitator tub, then hauled her sore and tired body into Grandma's kitchen for a well-deserved cup of coffee with a few other island ladies who came to witness the event.

After several hours of washing, rinsing, wringing and dumping out the dirty water, Mom reloaded the heavy wet clothes back on Grandpa's wheelbarrow, pushed it back down the rocky path, loaded clothes and kids back into the skiff for the long row home. She lugged the wet laundry back up to the house and the clotheslines where she hung it up to dry.

If a moose with antlers didn't get tangled in the clothesline and we kids stayed out from underfoot, she could start cooking supper for our cold, wet, tired and hungry dad, who shortly was due home off the lake.

Greenstoning

So you want to go greenstoning? I'm sworn to secrecy regarding beach locations, but I can give you a few tips to get you started. If you can't bribe a local old-timer by schmoozing, torture or snoose, you have to dope out the hot beaches yourself. Also, if you're hunting greenstones on Isle Royale, check Park Service regulations first. If the superintendent is a rock hound, you're in luck.

Gemstone quality greenstones, or chlorastrolite, are rarer than diamonds and rubies and are found only on Isle Royale, the Keweenaw Peninsula and in Madagascar. When polished they have a turtle-back pattern of various shades of green that has chatoyance or luster. Greenstones make gorgeous jewelry.

On Isle Royale, you'll need a small boat that can be pulled part way up on the beach. A cup-sized container, boat cushion and a garden tool would be handy as you inch your way down the beach at about l foot per hour. You'll resemble a pig rooting for truffles as you work bent over on all fours turning over every rock and piece of gravel in your search. You'll seldom find a gem-sized beach-polished stone. You'll find only flecks and parts of greenstone still embedded in the mother rock. Greenstone is slightly heavier than other stones its size.

When you find a beach with parts of green nodules embedded in lava, it could be a greenstone beach. The first greenstone you find will probably be where you pulled the boat onto the beach. It will suck you into a day of scraping, digging and moving rocks and boulders until your fingertips are raw, knees and elbows bloody and black fly and mosquito bites cover your sunburned body. But it's all worthwhile when you have your eureka moment and find your first ring- or pendant-sized stone. Don't let large spiders, worms, snakes and fresh moose tracks deter you from your quest.

While you eat your picnic lunch you'll have a chance to look up at your surroundings. Harebells, beach roses, raspberries, driftwood and sometimes a curious moose adorn the beach, making the adventure complete. During lunch you can spread out your possibilities on a handkerchief and determine which ones you'll grind and polish during the winter.

Next year when you flash that gorgeous greenstone ring, people will ask where you found it. You will have to lie … probably for the first time … and say that you found it at the Rock Harbor Lighthouse beach. It's the Isle Royale greenstoner's lie No. 1.

The End of a Beautiful Day

Lake Superior's moods can change from tranquility to terror in just a matter of minutes. More than 350 vessels have been lost to her terrible mood swings. More than 1,000 people lost their lives in those shipwrecks. The "big blow" of November 1913 alone stranded 19 ships; six were driven ashore as total losses while 12 others vanished completely.

Weather forecasting using modern technology has improved since the old days, but if captains ignore the warnings issued by the weather bureau and their own instruments, they could be heading into a disaster. While cruising down the beautiful dead-calm lake with not a cloud in the sky, it's difficult to take the fall in the barometer or the inclement weather warning on the ship's radio seriously. On November 6, 1975, the captain of the *Edmund Fitzgerald*, a giant 729-foot ore carrier, decided to ignore the weather forecast and his barometer that predicted a large storm approaching along his route. The gale turned into a 100-year mega storm that sank his ship with all 29 hands aboard.

Most commercial fishermen had barometers in their homes at Isle Royale. Reliable weather forecasts were not available over their AM radios in the 1930s and '40s, so they checked their barometers several times a day. But they, too, were susceptible to doubting the dip in the barometer on those gorgeous, sunny calm days of summer. They, too, got caught on the lake when the gales and monster storms hit, sometimes costing them their lives.

At times those rare storms hit so suddenly and with such velocity and without warning that it became impossible to turn the boat toward home, to a lee shore or a sheltered cove.

When heading into the seas, usually recommended as the best seamanship, or if running with the seas is impossible, the only option left is to run in the trough. By cutting the correct angle to the waves, surfboard like, it's possible to keep out from under the tumbling surf to arrive at shelter somewhere or to ride out the storm.

Viewing the lake while standing on shore, it is difficult to imagine the violence of which the lake is capable. While gazing out at beautiful, placid waters of Lake Superior sparkling in the sun on a normal summer's day, it is hard to comprehend seas that wash completely over giant ships or lighthouses standing 60 feet above the water's edge.

Late Haul Out

Commercial fishing on Isle Royale was just marginal from April until September. The fishing season was closed for several weeks in October to allow the trout to spawn. All hopes for a successful season depended on how long the fishermen could put out nets in November, when fish were plentiful. But every day in November, they risked losing all their nets to the dreaded storms or an early freeze-up. The temptation was to eke out just one more day to make out financially for the year.

Some years fishermen were caught in fast moving cold fronts called Canadian clippers that created ice in the shallow waters of sheltered coves. Heeding the warning of more cold and ice to come, they pulled in nets and hauled out the boats.

Helping each other, they usually managed to haul all the boats out in one day. Spirits were high with the thought of going back to the mainland, settling up and celebrating. Boats were pulled out using log rollers and block and tackle. Men tugged on the rope to "Heave-Hos" shouted in unison as boats inched forward to their final positions where they were propped up and covered with canvas. It didn't take long to pack up and be ready for the last freight boat of the season back to town.

In Duluth, they went to the fish company that financed their season and "settled up." The cost of their equipment, personal goods and sometimes groceries were deducted from the fish sold. If the fisherman were lucky enough to survive disastrous storms and catch a lot of fish, he'd earn enough to make it through the winter. If not, he'd have to work through the winter to pay his debt.

Some got jobs with the fish companies or worked in the woods or continued to fish herring in Duluth or on the north shore. A few bachelor fishermen took their payoff in cash, but in just a few days it was all invested in the bowery.

Most would tell you that was their last year on the "rock," but by spring they were anxious to "go to the island" at least one more time.

Heritage Lost

To lose one's heritage is a terrible thing. The young man sitting in his grandfather's old and rotting boat reminisces about the past and contemplates his future after losing his heritage on Isle Royale.

Commercial fishing was a family tradition brought over from Scandinavia in the late 1800s. His grandparents and relatives settled on Isle Royale and raised their children and grandchildren to harvest lake trout, whitefish and herring as food for tables throughout their new country.

The first blow to his heritage came when the government confiscated his home to create a primeval wilderness in the form of a national park, dedicated in 1945. His grandfather and father were allowed to continue fishing on a year-by-year basis. When they retired, the family home was bulldozed and burned, putting an end to his future on the island.

The final blow to his heritage came when two deadly predators of trout and whitefish entered the lake through the new St. Lawrence Seaway. It took just a few years for the blood-sucking lamprey eels that killed adult fish and the piranha-like rainbow smelt that devoured spawn, fry and fingerlings to decimate lake trout and whitefish. A sharp decline in herring at about the same time was the result of their spawning beds, on the western end of Lake Superior, being covered with taconite tailings from the new plant at Silver Bay. Along with the invasion of smelt, the herring population dropped drastically. By the time the young man in the boat returned from several years in the army, fighting for his country on the front lines in Korea, he came home to find his heritage gone.

After 30 years of heroic effort, the American and Canadian departments of natural resources finally got the lamprey and smelt under control and restocked the lake with hatchery-reared trout. Too late, however, for the lad in the boat whose island home is gone. The lake trout have been designated as a sport fish and reserved only for sport fishermen, leaving no present or future for commercial harvesting of that fish for food.

The recreational industry took the young man's home and livelihood so that others may hike and sport fish, putting an end to his heritage and dreams.

For Further Enlightenment

Selected Museums

Grand Portage National Monument
P.O. Box 426
Grand Portage, Minnesota 55605
(tel. 218-475-0123)
Stockade open daily mid-May to mid-October. The historic site of the Grand Portage post, with reconstructed stockade and Great Hall, exhibits, demonstrations, video programs, heritage center.

Fort William Historical Park
Vickers Heights PO
Thunder Bay, Ontario P0T 2Z0, Canada
(tel. 807-473-2344)
Open daily year-round; expanded activities mid-June to mid-August. Dozens of costumed interpreters in summer season recreating the life of a fur-trade post during rendezvous. Guided tours, canoe activities, dramatic reenactments, craft and trade demonstrations.

Books

Barbara Chisholm, Andrea Gutsche, Russell Floren. *Superior: In the Shadow of the Gods.* Lynx Images, Inc., 1998. *A history of Lake Sueprior's Canadian shore.*

Alexander Henry. *Travels and Adventures in Canada and the Indian Territories, 1760-1776.* Little, Brown & Company, 1901. *A fur trader's accounts of his travels, mishaps and transaction in his business.*

Grade Lee Nute. *The Voyageur.* St. Paul: Minnesota Historical Society, 1931. An engaging portrait of the French-Canadian canoemen and their songs and customs.

Grade Lee Nute. *The Voyageur's Highway: Minnesota's Border Lake Land.* St. Paul: Minnesota Historical Society, 1951. A historical guide to the Minnesota-Ontario canoe country, from Lake Superior to Rainy Lake.

Peter Oikarinen. *Island Folk: The People of Isle Royale.* Isle Royale Natural History Association, 1979. *The lives and history of Isle Royale's families with accompanying photos.*

Dr. Willis H. Raff. *Pioneers in the Wilderness.* Cook County Historical Society, 1981. *A history of Minnesota's Cook County, Grand Marais and the Gunflint in the 19th century.*

William W. Warren. *History of the Ojibway Nation.* Minneapolis, Ross & Haines, 1970. *A history of the Ojibway, based upon traditionas and oral statements.*

Periodicals

Lake Superior Magazine. Published bimonthly by Lake Superior Port Cities Inc., P.O. Box 16417, Duluth, Minnesota 55816-0417. (tel. 1-888-BIG LAKE [888-244-5253], 218-722-5002), www.lakesuperior.com.

About the Author
by the Author

I was raised as a member of the Sivertson Family's third generation of commercial fishermen on Isle Royale. My grandparents immigrated from Norway and settled at Washington Harbor in 1892. My father was born there in 1903 and I in 1930. I helped Dad harvest lake trout, whitefish and herring from the cold, clear waters surrounding the most beautiful island in the world. But I didn't help much. He would have had a much easier time of it without a seasick, clumsy, dreamy kid in the boat with him.

He was glad, I'm sure, when I came home from my first day in kindergarten at Merritt School in Duluth and announced my intention of becoming a famous artist. That day my teacher asked each kid "What did you do last summer?" as the usual ice breaker. I didn't understand the other kids' stories, never experiencing a summer on the mainland, and they didn't understand my stories of my summer in an island fishing community.

She asked if I would illustrate my strange stories on the blackboard to help understanding. After two hours of talking and drawing, I got a hug and a pat on my head. Why wouldn't I choose, then and there, to become an artist? It was the first time I'd received praise for my work and I didn't throw up once.

My interest in art was encouraged at Washington Junior High and Denfeld High School in Duluth and led to the Minneapolis School of Art and the University of Minnesota Duluth. I responded to the Korean War problem by joining the U.S. Navy and fighting for my country in Hawaii, drawing cartoons for publication in stateside newspapers.

My first daughter, Jan, was born in Hawaii in 1953. Son Jeff came along three years later and Liz three years after that in Duluth. After 25 years raising a family while working as a graphic artist in Duluth, I returned to my original goal of fine arts painting with Isle Royale, the Boundary Waters Canoe Area Wilderness and Lake Superior's north shore as my subjects.

Artist/daughter Jan owns art galleries in Grand Marais and Duluth where she exhibits artist/daughter Liz, artist/wife Elaine and artist/father Howard's paintings. Son Jeff works for the St. Louis County Highway Department, builds and reconditions wood boats and continues the family tradition of spending summers at Isle Royale on the Sivertson family homestead, which the National Park Service owns but leases to the family.

I continue to paint and write from my winter studio in Grand Marais, Minnesota, and my summer studio at Little Trout Bay among the Canadian islands just 14 miles across the lake from Isle Royale.

Driftwood is my fifth book of painted stories of Lake Superior and Boundary Waters history. *Once Upon An Isle, The Illustrated Voyageur, Tales of the Old North Shore* and *Schooners, Skiffs and Steamships* preceded it.

– Howard Sivertson
April 2008

From Lake Superior Port Cities Inc.

www.lakesuperior.com

Lake Superior Magazine (Bimonthly)

Lake Superior Travel Guide (Annual)

Hugh E. Bishop:

The Night the Fitz Went Down
Softcover: ISBN 978-0-942235-37-1

*By Water and Rail: A History of
Lake County, Minnesota*
Hardcover: ISBN 978-0-942235-48-7
Softcover: ISBN 978-0-942235-42-5

Haunted Lake Superior
Softcover: ISBN 978-0-942235-55-5

Haunted Minnesota
Softcover: ISBN 978-0-942235-71-5

*Lake Superior,
The Ultimate Guide to the Region*
Softcover: ISBN 978-0-942235-66-1

Bonnie Dahl:

*Bonnie Dahl's Superior Way,
Fourth Edition*
Softcover: ISBN 978-0-942235-92-0

Joy Morgan Dey, Nikki Johnson:

Agate: What Good Is a Moose?
Softcover: ISBN 978-0-942235-73-9

Daniel R. Fountain:

*Michigan Gold,
Mining in the Upper Peninsula*
Softcover: ISBN 978-0-942235-15-9

Marvin G. Lamppa:

Minnesota's Iron Country
Softcover: ISBN 978-0-942235-56-2

Daniel Lenihan:

*Shipwrecks of
Isle Royale National Park*
Softcover: ISBN 978-0-942235-18-0

Betty Lessard:

Betty's Pies Favorite Recipes
Softcover: ISBN 978-0-942235-50-0

James R. Marshall:

*Shipwrecks of Lake Superior,
Second Edition*
Softcover: ISBN 978-0-942235-67-8

*Lake Superior Journal:
Views from the Bridge*
Softcover: ISBN 978-0-942235-40-1

Howard Sivertson

*Driftwood:
Stories Picked Up Along the Shore*
Hardcover: ISBN 978-0-942235-91-3

*Schooners, Skiffs & Steamships:
Stories along Lake Superior's
Water Trails*
Hardcover: ISBN 978-0-942235-51-7

Tales of the Old North Shore
Hardcover: ISBN 978-0-942235-29-6

The Illustrated Voyageur
Hardcover: ISBN 978-0-942235-43-2

*Once Upon an Isle:
The Story of Fishing Families
on Isle Royale*
Hardcover: ISBN 978-0-962436-93-2

Frederick Stonehouse:

*Wreck Ashore: United States
Life-Saving Service,
Legendary Heroes of the
Great Lakes*
Softcover: ISBN 978-0-942235-58-6

Shipwreck of the Mesquite
Softcover: ISBN 978-0-942235-10-4

Haunted Lakes (the original)
Softcover: ISBN 978-0-942235-30-2

Haunted Lakes II
Softcover: ISBN 978-0-942235-39-5

Haunted Lake Michigan
Softcover: ISBN 978-0-942235-72-2

Haunted Lake Huron
Softcover: ISBN 978-0-942235-79-1

Julius F. Wolff Jr.:

*Julius F. Wolff Jr.'s
Lake Superior Shipwrecks*
Hardcover: ISBN 978-0-942235-02-9
Softcover: ISBN 978-0-942235-01-2